Sing for your Supper

NICK WARBURTON

Illustrated by Martin Cottam

PACIFIC
LEARNING

© 2001 Pacific Learning
© 1995 Written by **Nick Warburton**
Illustrated by **Martin Cottam**
US Edit by **Rebecca Weber McEwen**

This Americanized Edition of *Sing for Your Supper,*
originally published in English in 1995, is published
by arrangement with Oxford University Press.

05 04 03 02 01
10 9 8 7 6 5 4 3 2 1

Published by
Pacific Learning
P.O. Box 2723
Huntington Beach, CA 92647-0723
www.pacificlearning.com

ISBN: 1-59055-070-6
PL-7511

Contents

CHAPTER 1

Red Beard

The smell of meat pies woke Jamie. His nose twitched before his eyes opened.

Jamie's mother was dead. His father had gone to sea and not come back. He remembered the full white sails as the little galleon had moved out of Plymouth harbor, but he'd forgotten what his father looked like. For two years he'd lived on the streets and begged for his food. He was used to sniffing out food.

He'd been dozing on a pile of straw beside the horse trough when the pie man walked by with his tray.

Food, Jamie thought at once. *Warm, delicious food.*

He didn't have a coin to his name, but he followed the man anyway. He was heading for The Boar's Head.

Jamie saw him push his tray into the crowd at the door and disappear inside.

Jamie dropped to his knees and crawled through a forest of sturdy legs. Jamie's nose told him that the pie man had stopped by a table in the corner. Keeping an eye open for the innkeeper, he crawled on. The pie man had set two steaming pies on the table.

His customers weren't ordinary sailors. They wore stiff ruffled collars and fancy buttons down the front of their tunics. Jamie had seen one of them around Plymouth before – the one with the red curly hair and the pointed beard.

He must be important, Jamie thought, *but he looks like a man who might share his meal with a hungry boy.*

"No mutton pies after we set sail," the man with the red beard said to his friend. "Ship's biscuits and hard cheese and not much else."

"Maybe we'll get some Spanish gold to
spend when we get back, eh, Francis?"
his friend said.

Francis. So that was his name. And
Spanish gold. That meant battles at sea,
didn't it? Maybe they were pirates.

"Well, Master Francis," Jamie said to
himself, "I can't wait for your gold but I
would like to share part of your dinner."

He popped up from behind the table as the redheaded man was about to eat.

"May I sing you a song, Master Francis?" Jamie asked him.

Francis blinked at him.

"Please, Master," Jamie said. "A song for a mouthful of pie."

The man laughed and asked him if he had a good voice.

"A wonderful voice, sir. Sweet as the birds, I promise."

"If you want to earn the price of a pie," Francis's friend said, "you can go down to the harbor and help load our ship."

"What ship is that, sir?" Jamie asked.

"*The Pelican*. It's being loaded for a voyage to…"

Before he could say another word, Francis held up a hand to stop him.

"Quiet, Will," he said. "A busy inn is not the place to talk about our plans."

Will looked around the noisy room. Jamie looked around too. Sure enough – or so he thought – there was a thin man at the next table, leaning toward them as if to catch every word. When Jamie's eye met his, the man scowled at him.

That face could sour milk, Jamie thought. It was full of trouble. After two years on the streets, Jamie knew trouble when he saw it.

A shiver of fear ran up his spine, but then Francis was speaking to him again.

"Come on, lad," he said. "Sing away."

Jamie opened his mouth to sing, but a broad hand grabbed his neck and he felt himself jerked off his feet.

"I've told you before," boomed a voice. "You leave my gentlemen in peace."

It was the innkeeper. He crooked an arm around Jamie's throat and crushed him against his greasy apron.

Jamie kicked and flailed his arms but it was no use. The innkeeper hauled him to the door and tossed him into the night.

He landed in the street. Instead of the smell of mutton, his nose was filled with the stench of straw and horse dung. It was the second time he'd been thrown out of The Boar's Head that night.

He stood up and shook himself. Across the street he saw the glow of candlelight from The Swan. The hum of voices inside tempted him to try his luck there, but he'd been thrown out of The Swan too.

Jamie didn't feel like being dumped in horse muck a fourth time.

"Oh well," he mumbled as he dusted himself off, "maybe I *should* go down to the harbor. If they're loading for a voyage, maybe I can pick up some scraps."

Soon he heard the lap of water against
wooden hulls and ropes slapping in the
breeze. He saw masts swaying against
the blue-black sky. The ship in front of
him was *The Pelican*. There were others
too, lined up behind it.

The harbor was busy for that time of night. Dark figures with sacks on their shoulders hurried back and forth. Some dumped their loads on the wall and others tottered up planks onto the ships.

He stopped one of the sailors and asked if he could help.

"Get out of here, little 'un," the sailor growled. "You'll only get in our way."

Jamie sighed and sat down in the shadow of a wall. His stomach grumbled with hunger in the dark. His head hurt. He watched the men loading their stores. He'd seen ships being loaded many times. Once he'd seen a sack drop and split open, sending cheeses rolling over the cobbles.

A good round cheese would taste awfully good now, he thought. *Maybe someone will drop a few sacks tonight.* Sack after sack he saw carried onto the ships, but no one stumbled and nothing spilled.

At last the men stopped work and went off together, laughing and joking.

For a while Jamie sat there. Then he stood up and stretched.

He was about to wander back into Plymouth Town when something caught his eye.

Two of the men came back. Or were they the same men? It was too dark to see very well, and they were wrapped in long cloaks.

They moved like the men who'd loaded the ships, trotting along with their heads bowed. Still, there was something different about them.

At first Jamie couldn't think what it was. Then it came to him. They had no sacks on their backs. They were running up the plank onto *The Pelican,* but they carried no stores. He saw them drop into the ship and disappear in shadow. Jamie sat down again and waited.

A man with a lantern on a pole came wandering along. It was the watchman, keeping his eye on the ships with their load of fresh stores. He walked steadily along the harbor wall until he reached the ship farthest from *The Pelican*. Then he paused for a moment before turning around. That was when the two men came scuttling down the plank again.

One was tall with pale hands that fluttered in the dark. Jamie knew him. It was the sour-faced man from The Boar's Head. The other man was short and thickset.

They moved nimbly and silently, and this time they were carrying something. At least, the short one was. It was in a black bag, and the short man carried it on his shoulder like a barrel.

Jamie shrank back into the shadow of a wall. He saw the men look around and spot the watchman. The tall man picked up a stone in his pale hands.

He hurled it high over the masts of *The Pelican*, and Jamie heard it drop into the sea with a deep splash.

Along the harbor wall the watchman heard it too. He spun around and held himself still. Then he lifted his lantern and peered between the ships, trying to see where the sound had come from.

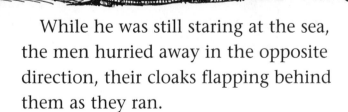

While he was still staring at the sea, the men hurried away in the opposite direction, their cloaks flapping behind them as they ran.

20

CHAPTER 2

Pale Hands

Jamie's mind was racing. He knew that something odd was going on. He waited until the men were almost out of sight, then set off after them. When they turned into a side street, he forced himself to run faster.

I must not lose them now, he thought as he pounded along. *They'll disappear down some dark alley. I must keep up.*

Jamie had seen plenty of thieves on the streets, but these two were different and he was sure they were dangerous. Common sense told him to stay out of it, but he was curious. Also, maybe there was the chance of pleasing Red Beard and earning some food – or maybe even something better than food.

"I must not lose them," he muttered over and over. "I must not lose them."

As soon as the men reached the safety of a side street, they stopped running to catch their breath.

They were bending down to examine the thing in the black bag, when Jamie hurtled around the corner and ran straight into them.

He fell over one and crashed into the other. There were rough shouts, the rustle of cloaks, and a waving of arms.

Jamie's struggle didn't last long.

Soon he felt a knee on his chest and long fingers tightening on his arm. He twisted his head and saw the same pale hand that had thrown the stone into the water. There was a silver ring on the middle finger. A face came close and spoke to him in a harsh voice.

"Where do you think you're going?"

The short, heavy man was the one who was kneeling on him, and the stench of his breath made Jamie flinch.

"I'm sorry, sir," he said. "I'm sorry."

Then the tall man spoke and his voice was a thin whisper.

"He's following us, Tom. I saw him talking to Red Beard in The Boar's Head."

"No, sir," Jamie said. "I'm not following you – I'm running away. Honest. The watchman's after me."

The fingers loosened on Jamie's arm and the men darted a look at each other. They glanced nervously back at the corner of the street.

They only looked away for a second, but it was enough for Jamie. He wriggled from under Tom's knee and scrambled to his feet.

The men grabbed at him, missed, and he went charging off into the darkness.

"Hey! Come back here!" Tom shouted
after him.

Jamie dived into an alley and banged
his shin against something he couldn't
see. From the way it clattered against
the wall behind him, he guessed it was
an empty barrel. The men came
lumbering after him, and one of them
kicked the barrel too.

Jamie came to a gap between two houses and ran blindly into it, hoping nothing would be in his way this time. Luckily, there wasn't.

He groped along a wall until he found a low fence. He swung himself over it and dropped into a little garden.

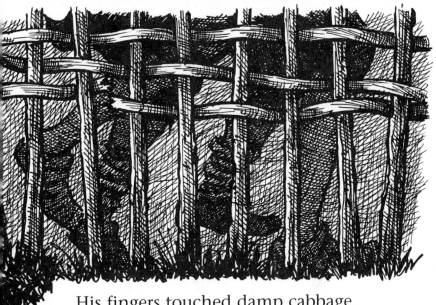

His fingers touched damp cabbage leaves and a fish head. He crouched there wide-eyed, trying to still his harsh breathing.

Heavy feet thudded by him, only yards away. The sound disappeared into the night, and then there was silence. He waited. A dog barked in the distance. A sharp pain began to throb in his leg. He hadn't noticed it when he was running.

After two or three more minutes, he let out a long sigh and painfully climbed out of the garden.

"You should use your nose for sniffing out food, Jamie," he told himself, "and keep clear of bad men in long cloaks."

He imagined what the men might do if they caught him. The thought made him shudder.

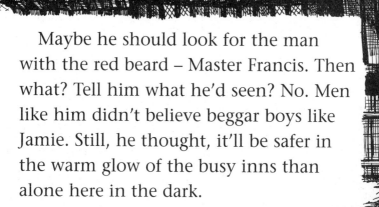

Maybe he should look for the man with the red beard – Master Francis. Then what? Tell him what he'd seen? No. Men like him didn't believe beggar boys like Jamie. Still, he thought, it'll be safer in the warm glow of the busy inns than alone here in the dark.

So he rubbed his leg and walked slowly through backstreets and alleyways toward the heart of the town. After a while he found himself outside The Boar's Head again.

"Well, here I am again," Jamie said out loud, "and I'm worse off than I was before. Still, I'll be safe and warm in here, as long as I keep my head down."

He slid in at the door and looked around cautiously.

The place was full, and noisy with talk and laughter. Jamie hoped he might be able to scrounge a scrap of bread. He squeezed onto the nearest bench and made himself as small as he could.

The men next to him kept their backs turned and talked in low voices. Jamie could see two empty plates on the table in front of them. There wasn't even a scrap of bread, though, so he soon lost interest in them.

He was looking around for more promising customers when one of the men reached out to pick up his mug.

Jamie turned and looked, then looked again, and his heart gave a sudden lurch.

The man's hand was long and pale, with a silver ring on the middle finger.

CHAPTER 3

A Bit of Bread and Cheese

"I told you, Tom," Jamie heard the thin man say. "The boy was in here talking to Red Beard. He was watching *The Pelican*. He must be a spy."

"What if he is?" Tom said shortly. "We've got what we were after, Jack. Anyway, if we see him again I'll take care of him. No need to worry."

"If, Tom. If we see him again."

"Stop harping on it. A scrap of a kid like that can't harm us."

The man named Jack sighed and shook his head. He banged the mug down on the table so hard it made Jamie jump.

What if they catch me? Jamie thought. *Nobody will care. I've got to get out of here.*

He glanced quickly at the open door. There were three or four people standing by it, laughing as if they didn't have a care in the world.

Just then Tom coughed and leaned over to spit on the floor. Jamie caught a glimpse of his broad face and his heart began to pound in his chest.

Run, he thought. *Run now, Jamie!* As he turned to flee, a huge sailor with thick brass rings through his ears plomped down beside him.

He was trapped, squashed between the sailor and thin-faced Jack.

His head began to spin and points of candlelight swam before his eyes. Jack had seen him. His mouth dropped open – a mouth studded with two black teeth.

"You," Jack said in a whispery voice.

His strong hand grabbed Jamie by the shoulder and squeezed. Jamie squirmed but could not break free.

His face was white with fear. The big sailor nudged him fiercely and told him to sit still.

"Look what we've got here, Tom," Jack hissed in a cruel voice.

Tom blinked with shock at the sight of Jamie sitting there. Then he started to chuckle and rub his hands together with satisfaction.

That terrified Jamie. He opened his mouth and a thin, squeaking sound came out.

"Shut up," Jack snapped, shaking Jamie's shoulder.

The sailor turned to look at Jamie.

"What's wrong with him?" he asked.

"Nothing," Jack said with a sickly smile. "He's just singing us a little song, aren't you, lad?"

Jamie nodded. Just singing. Singing for his supper. He took a breath and began to sing in a wavery voice. He couldn't think of a tune so he made one up.

"A bit of b-b-bread and cheese is all I ask," he sang. "All I ask is a bit of b-b-bread and cheese."

"Take him outside," Tom growled. "Right now!"

I'm in serious trouble, Jamie thought.
I'm in really serious trouble.

Still, he went on singing. Then he saw the innkeeper pushing his way through the crowd toward them.

"You again!" he bellowed. "How many times do I have to tell you not to bother my customers?"

He reached across the table and grabbed Jamie by the front of his tunic. People looked around and cheered as the innkeeper lifted him off the bench and swung him into the air.

"Let him be!" the sailor laughed. "He only wants to sing."

The innkeeper dropped Jamie, and he clattered to the floor and crawled under the table. He felt his head bump into something. At first he thought it was someone's knee, but it made a hollow sound against his head. Then Tom's head appeared beneath the table. He snarled and lunged at Jamie. Jamie lurched backward. Someone caught hold of his ankles and he felt himself being dragged belly-down across the floor.

It's Jack, he thought. *He's got me!*

It wasn't Jack. It was the innkeeper, and he was hauling Jamie to the door.

Everyone shouted and cheered as he
dropped Jamie to the ground and shoved
him into the street.

Jamie skidded and tripped, then jumped up and ran. He ran until he reached the corner of the street. When he looked back, he saw Tom and Jack, stuck in the doorway of The Boar's Head, trying to shove their way out. Their faces were twisted with rage.

He tried to keep going, but his legs were weak with fright and running wasn't easy.

He looked down and found that he was still clutching the black thing he'd found under the table.

He peered down at it and froze in his tracks.

"Unbelievable!" he whispered. "How did I get out of there with this?"

Then he took off.

CHAPTER 4

Out of the Black Bag

Jamie swung the bundle over his
shoulder and bolted. As he ran he could
hear a hollow sound thumping against
his back. Something was rattling too.

What could it be? What kind of
treasure rattled like that?

He heard Tom and Jack racing up
and down the streets behind him. This
time, though, he had a good start.

Five minutes later, after twisting and turning down narrow lanes, he lost them completely. At last he came to a churchyard and slipped in among the graves. He found a spot behind a tall headstone and fell to his knees to rest.

The night was now thick and dark, but a little light filtered down from a sliver of moon. He set the bag down and examined it.

It was tied at the top with a piece of white cord. His fingers fiddled nervously at the knot, and he pulled the black cloth away. A pale disc appeared. He touched it gently. It felt like paper or tight leather, and it made a soft booming sound.

It was a drum.

Jamie was disappointed. A drum and a couple of drumsticks. They must have been what made the rattling sound. All that fuss for an old drum! He kicked it away in disgust.

"I thought it was treasure," he groaned. "I thought it was important. A stupid old drum! What use is that?"

He left the drum and picked up the black cloth bag. Then he wrapped it around his shoulders. He leaned against the headstone and closed his eyes.

"This is more useful than a stupid old drum," he grumbled. "At least this'll keep me warm."

He yawned and thought about his night's work: all those times getting thrown out of the inn, all that running away from men in cloaks. What was it about, and where had it gotten him? Alone in a graveyard with a worthless drum. A worthless drum in a lonely graveyard. The words tumbled over and over in his head, and a minute or two later he was fast asleep.

Drops of cold rain on his face and a
pattering sound woke him. There was a
stiff pain in his neck as he sat up. He
blinked in the morning light. The drum
was still where he'd kicked it. Raindrops
were bouncing off it.

He scowled at it. He sat there staring
at it and thinking. What in the world
should he do with it?

He could smash it up and make a little fire with it – it might warm him for ten minutes or so. He could take it to the market and try to sell it, although if he took it to the market, he might end up being chased through every street in Plymouth again.

"It's useless," he muttered.

Still, it looked a little more impressive in the daylight. It was not an ordinary drum. It was well made and brightly painted with little pictures. After all, Tom and Jack had stolen it from *The Pelican*, and they must have thought it was worth something.

I'll have to take it back, he thought. *Someone will be pleased to see it. Of course, Tom and Jack might catch me with it, but that's a chance I'll have to take.*

He got up and stretched and shivered.

"That's what I'll do," he said out loud. "I'll take it back."

50

CHAPTER 5

A Good Turn

The harbor was again bustling with activity when he arrived. The last of the supplies were being loaded. One or two richly dressed men were pacing up and down, directing sailors who trotted up gangplanks with sacks and barrels.

"These barrels of tar are for *The Pelican*!" someone shouted. "Don't forget candles! More candles and cloth aboard *The Marigold*! Move yourselves!"

Jamie watched as men clung to masts and spars, tightening ropes and checking sails. Gulls circled and screamed above.

After a while Jamie stopped in front of a short, fat sailor with his head bent forward under a heavy sack.

"Please, master," he began, but the sailor only growled at him.

"Please, may I ask you something?" Jamie persisted.

The sailor squinted at Jamie, swayed under his load, then shouted, "Out of my way, you brat! Can't you see we're busy?"

"Pig!" Jamie muttered after him as he moved away.

It's no use asking men with stores to carry, he realized; better to ask someone coming off the ships empty-handed.

"Excuse me, master, but I've got something here…"

The empty-handed sailors didn't want to know either, and *they* had their hands free to take a swipe at anyone who dared to get in their way.

The fine gentlemen who were shouting out orders only wrinkled their noses at him and waved him away.

"Out of the way, boy! Out of the way!"

"Don't any of you want to see what I have here?" Jamie shouted at them.

Nobody did. They bustled around, running and carrying and shouting, and they completely ignored him. He sighed heavily and sat on a low wall with the drum on his lap.

What could he do with it now? He couldn't sell it in the market and he couldn't give it back. What would they want with a drum on a long voyage anyway? They'd need tar and candles, beef and pork, biscuits and cloth – but a drum? Even a fancy drum like this one was of no use to anyone.

He folded back the cloth and looked at the drum. One of the sticks dropped at his feet and he picked it up. He tapped it lightly against the tight skin. It made a deep, pleasing sound. He found the other stick and gave the drum a couple of rattling blows. Yes, that sounded impressive.

He tapped sharply with the sticks, trying to beat a rhythm like the street musicians always played.

A rat-a-tat-tat BONG BONG!

A rat-a-tat-tat BONG BONG!

When he stopped, the drum echoed into silence. In fact, the whole harbor seemed quiet now. The shouting had stopped, and he couldn't hear the pounding of feet on planks anymore. He looked up.

The sailors and the men in their rich clothes were standing still and staring at him. Then one or two began to move. They walked slowly toward him. Jamie gazed from face to face and swallowed. Soon he seemed to be surrounded by hundreds of men, all of them looking at him, all of them waiting.

"What?" he said quietly. "What is it?"

A short man with curly red hair was pushing his way through the crowd. The others moved aside to let him pass. He stopped in front of Jamie and frowned down at him.

Jamie knew him. It was the one he thought of as Red Beard. Master Francis.

"What do you have there, young man?" he asked quietly.

"It's a drum," Jamie stammered. "It was stolen from *The Pelican* and I brought it back."

"Did you steal it?"

"No, sir. I saw two men run off with it. They were a thin man named Jack and an ugly one named Tom. I got it away from them and brought it back and... and..."

"And you've done me a good turn," Francis said. "In fact, you've done your country a good turn. Those men were enemies of Queen Elizabeth. They were spies, working for Spain. They'd do anything to keep me from setting out in *The Pelican*."

"Umm, master," Jamie said, "it's only an old drum..."

"No, no, lad. It's my drum. It's Drake's drum, and it brings me luck. I can't set sail without it."

Drake! Drake's drum. Jamie caught his breath. Of course! Francis of the red beard. Why didn't he think of it before? Everyone in Plymouth knew about Francis Drake – the great explorer.

"Drake's drum is more than just a drum," Francis was saying. "When my men hear the beat of my drum they know I'm near and they rally around. That drum is the hope of England."

The hope of England – and Jamie had nearly used it for firewood!

"What's your name, my boy?"

"Jamie."

"What work do you do, Jamie?"

"No work, sir. I have to beg for food."

Francis Drake turned to one of the men and waved his hand.

"Take the drum to my cabin. Bring
young Jamie too. He's a good, brave lad;
just the sort to be my cabin boy."

Suddenly everyone started talking
and laughing at once, and Jamie was
being led toward *The Pelican*. Hands
reached out to ruffle his hair and slap
him on the back.

A good, brave lad, he thought as he was jostled along. *Me. Jamie. I've done a good turn for my country, and there's better work for me than begging.* As cabin boy on *The Pelican*, Jamie knew that he would be in line for a share in any Spanish gold they acquired during their journey, and then...

Food! he thought, *as much food as I can eat!*

NOTE

Francis Drake set sail from Plymouth, England in *The Pelican* – which was later renamed *The Golden Hind* – on December 13, 1577. He led a small fleet that included *The Elizabeth*, *The Marigold*, *The Swan*, and *The Benedict*. Drake was said to have loved music, and some say he always traveled with a drum that he used to rally his men to him.

Few people knew his destination when he set out, but by the time he returned, nearly three years later, he had sailed around the world – the first Englishman to do so.

The men who returned from this amazing journey with him – including the cabin boy – were made rich by the voyage.

About the Author

I now live in a town called Cambridge in England, but I was born in Essex and I still follow the fortunes of Essex sports with great interest.

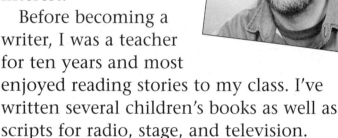

Before becoming a writer, I was a teacher for ten years and most enjoyed reading stories to my class. I've written several children's books as well as scripts for radio, stage, and television.

I think Francis Drake must have been a fascinating character. I still remember a poem called *Drake's Drum*, which I learned when I was about ten.

Nick Warburton